MW01006806

Choose
JOY
WOMEN'S DEVOTIONAL

Choose
JOY

WOMEN'S
DEVOTIONAL

Finding Joy
NO MATTER WHAT
You're Going Through

KAY WARREN

Revell

a division of Baker Publishing Group
Grand Rapids, Michigan

© 2015 by Kay Warren

Published by Revell
a division of Baker Publishing Group
PO Box 6287, Grand Rapids, MI 49516-6287
www.revellbooks.com

Repackaged edition published 2020
ISBN 978-0-8007-3827-3

Previously published in 2015 under the title *Choose Joy Devotional*

Printed in the United States of America

The Library of Congress has cataloged the original edition as follows:
Warren, Kay, 1954–
    Choose joy devotional : finding joy no matter what you're going through / Kay Warren.
        pages cm
    ISBN 978-0-8007-2440-5 (cloth)
    1. Joy—Religious aspects—Christianity—Meditations.
I. Title.
BV4647.J68W374 2015
242—dc23   2015007820

20 21 22 23 24 25 26   7 6 5 4 3 2 1

Contents

CONTENTS

Preface

When I wrote *Choose Joy: Because Happiness Isn't Enough*, I revealed that I had a close family member who was living with a mental illness. I spoke about the challenge of choosing joy in the face of a struggle that was very dark and scary at times—both for my loved one and for me. As you may know, our "struggle" became catastrophic loss when our twenty-seven-year-old son, Matthew, took his life in April of 2013 after two decades of intense, painful—even torturous—mental and emotional suffering. The news of his suicide seemed to fill the airwaves for a short period of time, and we were thrust into the public spotlight in ways we had always hoped to avoid.

The detailed circumstances of his death are private, but what I am comfortable telling you is that on the morning of April 5, 2013, I had very good reasons to believe he had taken his life, although it wouldn't be confirmed until later that day. The night before I did not sleep, full of anxiety and grief because I was pretty sure Matthew had died. So when I got dressed that morning, I deliberately reached into my jewelry drawer and selected a necklace that said *Choose Joy*. I was sick to my stomach, shaking from head to toe and terrified that what I had dreaded had actually happened. But I put it on because somewhere in the dim recesses of my frozen mind I was certain the only thing that would allow me to survive the loss of my son was what I knew and believed about God . . . and joy. That morning I possessed these three things: the settled assurance that God is in control of all the details of my life, the quiet confidence that *ultimately* everything is going to be okay, and the determined choice to give my praise to God—even on April 5, 2013.

These ensuing months of shattering grief and loss have severely tested those three convictions, and the opportunities to choose joy—or not—have been endless. I really believe that God allowed me to write *Choose Joy* before Matthew died to prepare me for what was ahead, so that when he died, I had the tools I desperately needed to survive and even thrive during one of life's most tragic losses.

Most of you will not face anything as devastating as the loss of a child due to suicide, but every single day you will face *something* that threatens your attempts to live with joy. Health problems, financial worries, marriage issues, loneliness, unresolved relational conflicts, anxiety about our nation or our world, stress over how your kids are turning out—the devil is at work nonstop to interfere with or interrupt your plans and dreams. Your primary task in life is to get to know God intimately and to send your spiritual roots deep into the soil of his love; to develop convictions and certainties about him that will become the source of your strength when happiness isn't enough.

I pray that these brief daily conversations about how to Choose Joy—No Matter What You're Going Through—will inspire you to know God better, to trust him more, and to become convinced that you, too, can choose joy!

The Definition of Joy

He will yet fill your mouth with laughter and
your lips with shouts of joy.

—Job 8:21

*H*ave you ever found yourself thinking,
*Is joy really possible for messed-up
and mixed-up people like me? Isn't joy just
a biblical word that has nothing to do with
real life?* Those are great questions—and just
the kind I ask myself. You see, finding joy is
a challenge for me. I'm not naturally an "up"
person; I'm more of a melancholy. In fact, I've
struggled with low-level depression as far back
as I can remember. Even as a little girl, I felt the
weight of the world on my shoulders. So when I

ask myself about joy, it's not from the perspective of one of those happy, peppy people who never has a down day. Some days I'm thrilled to just survive! It's really because of my own inability to live with joy that I began to study and explore why my experiences often didn't match up with Scripture.

One of the first things I realized as I studied Scripture is that the Bible gives some commands that are extremely hard to understand—and even harder to live out. And one of the hardest commands is the one found in James 1:2: "When troubles of any kind come your way, consider it an opportunity for great joy" (NLT).

Are you kidding me? When trouble comes my way, my first thoughts aren't usually about experiencing great joy. My typical reaction is more along the lines of fear, panic, worry, and even hopelessness.

And yet in Scripture I read about the life of Jesus Christ, the lives of people such as King David; Mary, the mother of Jesus; the apostle Paul; and James, the half brother of Jesus. I read how they reacted to trouble and sorrow and hard times. And when I read about their lives, it is clear that joy—even in pain—is something we as Christians can expect to experience on a regular basis.

In my struggle to match my reality with the truth of Scripture, I've realized part of the problem was my definition of joy. I thought that joy was "feeling good all the time." And truly, that's impossible. Even for those of you who are more naturally upbeat and optimistic, feeling good doesn't always happen. So if my *definition* wasn't accurate, there was no way I could experience joy.

You and I have to start someplace more realistic, more true to Scripture, and more attainable for all of us. A few years ago I read a quote that said joy is knowing that God is in control of our lives. I liked it, but I wanted more—I needed to put more words around it to give the complete picture. So here's what I've come up with from studying Scripture:

Joy is the settled assurance that God is in control of all the details of my life, the quiet

confidence that ultimately everything is going
to be all right, and the determined choice to
praise God in all things.

There's nothing in that definition about happy
feelings, because as we all know, happiness is
fleeting.

I also realized I had the wrong picture of a
life of joy, and maybe you do too. We tend to
think that life comes in hills and valleys, a se-
ries of good things and bad things happening
to us. But really it's much more like train tracks.
Every day of your life, delightful things happen.
Things that bring pleasure and contentment and
beauty. *At the exact same time*, however, there
are painful things that happen to you or those
you love; things that are disappointing, hurtful,
and even full of sorrow. These two tracks—joy
and sorrow—run parallel to each other every
single moment of your life. So while you are experiencing something amazing, there is the nag-
ging realization that it's not perfect . . . and while
you're experiencing something painful, there's
the glorious realization that there is still beauty

and loveliness to be found. They are inseparable, always running right next to each other.

Our goal, then, is not to figure out how to live only on the joy side of the tracks and avoid the sorrow side, but it's how to live on the parallel tracks where joy and sorrow run side by side. I don't know if you've realized it or not, but when you look into the brightness of the horizon, the tracks become one, no longer distinguishable as two separate tracks.

And that's the way it will be for us too. One day, these parallel tracks of joy and sorrow will merge into one. The day we meet Jesus Christ in person and see the brightness of who he is, it will all come together for us . . . the sorrow will disappear forever and only the joy will remain. And it will *all* make complete sense. Until then, we live with both joy and sorrow.

Will you pray with me?

Father, I want to choose joy in my life. Rekindle hope in my heart. Help me to keep seeking the joy that belongs to me in Jesus Christ. In his name, amen.

The Book of Joy

Yahweh your God is there with you, the warrior-Saviour. He will rejoice over you with happy song, he will renew you by his love, he will dance with shouts of joy for you.

—Zephaniah 3:17 NJB

What stops us from experiencing joy daily? One major roadblock is a misconception about God's Word. Most people think the Bible is a heartless, joyless collection of dry rules and regulations. But it's really a book of joy! Did you know that in the NIV translation of the Bible there are more than 500 references to joy, gladness, merriment, rejoicing, delighting, and laughing? And given the amount of suffering in the Bible, you would think there would be ten times as many negative references—words such as sad, sadness, mourning, and tears. But there are only 158 references. That tells us God's Word is a book of joy!

Another major roadblock to experiencing joy is our misconception about Jesus and God himself. What do you think the answer would be if you asked your friends, "Does God smile?" Most people perceive God as an angry, judgmental being who roams around looking for ways to squash all of our fun. Smile? Not a chance. All you have to do is look at artwork through the ages to know we have a skewed view of God. God is usually portrayed as a white-haired old codger with a beard. I admit, it's rather daunting to try to depict Almighty God accurately, especially since no one has ever seen him before! But Jesus—wow—there's a plethora of art dedicated to portraying Jesus, and much of it shows him in his time of terrible suffering, hanging bloodied and broken on the cross.

The Bible calls Jesus a "man of sorrows" in Isaiah 53—someone who was familiar with

17

grief and suffering. And it's true—the *role* Father God gave to Jesus was to be the Savior, the Redeemer of mankind, and that required horrific suffering and the shedding of his blood in a violent way. But when this is the primary image in our mind, we wrongly conclude that Jesus was *only* a man of sorrows—with little to no capacity for gladness, pleasure, and joy. We forget that he was in his *essence*, his nature, God. And God is a God of joy.

In the verse I quoted from the book of Zephaniah, God doesn't just smile—he sings and dances with shouts of joy—for you! My friend, he knows all about you. He knows how often you fail to get it right; he knows the truest intentions of your heart . . . he knows what no one else will ever know. And his response to all he sees within you . . . within me? This makes me weep. *He dances for us with shouts of joy.* This is the God I want a watching world to know through me.

I love the Phillips translation of Luke 7:34: "Then the Son of Man came, enjoying life."

It doesn't say the Son of Man came weeping copiously. Or the Son of Man came bent over in pain. Or the Son of Man came with a scowl on his face. It says the Son of Man came *enjoying life*. That blows my mind . . . and messes with my stereotype of Jesus as a killjoy or a man who couldn't survive without his box of Kleenex. He came eating and drinking—"feasting," says the Message paraphrase. That sounds like a man who experienced joy as well as sorrow. He sounds like someone I'd like to get to know! If he could experience joy, maybe I can too . . . and maybe you can as well. And a watching world will see us live out the truth about God—that he is a God of joy, the Bible is a book of joy, and Jesus was a man of joy.

Will you pray with me?

Father, help me to remember your delight in me. Help me not to focus on the ways I fail to accurately represent you. Help me to draw closer to you so that I can build a stronger faith-life that includes joy in all things. In Jesus's name, amen.

Jesus, Man of Joy

I have told you this so that my joy may be in you and that your joy may be complete.

—John 15:11

*T*hink about your perceptions of Jesus—is he mostly the Man of Sorrows, or can you also begin to see him as the Man of Joy? I know it can be weird to think of him laughing, smiling, rolling around on the ground with children, making jokes to his disciples, eating his favorite food, smelling bad after a long walk in the hot sun, or getting indigestion; the way we usually see him illustrated has limited our view of him and minimized his humanity.

But we can recover our view of Jesus as a Man of Joy. I think there are three simple ways to do this: we can look at his attitudes, his words, and his actions.

The Scriptures don't portray Jesus as a handsome man—in fact, Isaiah 53:2 says, "He wasn't some handsome king. Nothing about the way he looked made him attractive to us" (CEV). So there was nothing about him physically that drew people to him. He probably didn't have a handsome face or a gorgeous body—it wasn't his physical presence that attracted crowds to him. But they *were* attracted to him because of his attitude and demeanor.

For example, little kids loved him—and kids are usually a pretty good judge of who's cool to be with. My grandkids swarm all over Rick because he plays hard with them—tickles them, throws them up in the air, makes silly jokes—and they love it. Jesus consistently had children around him—and that says something about him.

Also, we all know that dull, boring people don't usually get a lot of party invitations. Yet

Jesus was invited to parties! He had a presence, an attractive personality, and people liked to have him around.

And by the way, Jesus was funny—I mean *really* funny. We just don't see the humor in his words, because first of all, we read the Bible like we're reading the phone book—boring, boring, boring! So we miss the laugh lines and often the cultural context. Jesus was a Jewish man talking mostly to other Jews, and he used humor by exaggeration. So when he told his disciples to stop judging each other—"take the log out of your own eye before you take the speck of dust out of your neighbor's eye"—it was very funny, and it communicated well!

Jesus's way of interacting with people showed his humanity and his sense of joy. One time, the apostle Peter saw Jesus walking on water in the middle of the night and decided to jump out of the boat and join him. As long as he kept his eyes on Jesus, Peter was able to walk on the water, but the second he looked down at the waves, he began to sink. Jesus rescued him immediately—and we typically interpret his words like this: "Oh Peter! You *idiot*! You have such teensy, weensy faith! DIDN'T YOU KNOW I WOULD CATCH YOU?"

I think he probably spoke with familiarity, gentleness, and affection: "Peter, Peter . . . you of little faith—didn't you know I would catch you?"

There's no doubt about Jesus's role and his mission here on earth: he came to die. In that role, he bore our sorrows and suffering upon himself. But he also came reflecting the joy, kindness, patience, and loveliness of God his Father—and as such, he was the Man of Joy.

This picture of Jesus is attractive to me. It makes him someone I can identify with. He was someone who knew what it was like to experience pain and betrayal and immense suffering, but he was also someone who could laugh and play and enter fully into life with all its brokenness. His life gives me permission to seek a life of joy for myself.

Today, I'm asking God to make me a woman of joy instead of a woman of sorrows. Do you need to ask him to do that for you too?

Will you pray with me?

Thank you for showing me, Jesus, that you are a full-of-joy kind of savior. Thank you for showing me that even in sorrow I can know blessings and joy and laughter. Teach me what it means to choose joy. In your precious name, amen.

Our True Colors

Consider it a sheer gift, friends, when tests
and challenges come at you from all sides.

—James 1:2 MSG

The Bible says something very interesting in James 1:2–4 in the Message paraphrase: "Consider it a sheer gift, friends, when
tests and challenges come at you from all sides.
You know that under pressure, your faith-life is
forced into the open and shows its true colors.
So don't try to get out of anything prematurely.
Let it do its work so you become mature and
well-developed, not deficient in any way."

I find it compelling that the passage says
in tough times, our "faith-life is *forced* into

the open and shows its true colors" (emphasis mine). Which means, I guess it doesn't matter what I *say* I believe about God, or what I *say* I believe about living a life of faith and joy, because what I really believe will be obvious to everyone—especially to me—when truly horrible things happen to us. It can be shocking to realize that your faith isn't as strong or deep as you thought it was.

There's no hiding or pretending when the bottom falls out—when you get bad news, or have a health scare, or someone dies, or your finances collapse, or your kids decide to make a mess out of their lives, or someone goes to prison, or mental illness destroys a relationship, or life itself seems meaningless and empty. All our great words and statements of faith are worthless when it all falls apart; what matters in those times is what we *do*.

So what do we do in those moments?

Back we go to James 1, which says to consider it a sheer gift when tests and challenges come at you from all sides. Another version of James 1 says, "Count it all joy, my brothers and sisters." As I've already said, joy is rarely my first reaction. I can probably count on one hand the number of times I've been initially successful at considering hard times a "gift" or "counted it all joy."

No, I'm just like you. My first reaction is usually anger or despair or bitterness—not joy, not thanking God for this "gift." And when I see that kind of a reaction in myself, I get disappointed in how far I still have to go to be a mature woman of God.

But that's exactly the point James is making. We hate the process, even though we all want the end product: spiritual maturity. The process that makes us like Christ involves pain and sorrow and stress and upheaval. And James says not to try and wriggle out of the hard times too soon; if we do, we will short-circuit the process and remain immature little babies.

I don't want to be a spiritual or emotional baby—do you? Of course not. Although in all honesty, there have been times when I've said, "God, I'm okay with staying a spiritual baby because growing is going to hurt!"

But in my heart of hearts, that's not what I want. I want my faith-life to be sturdy and strong, mature and well-developed. I'm willing to let trials and troubles expose my faith-life so I'll know to stay on the path until I'm finished. I want my true colors to show. I know you do too.

Will you pray with me?

Father, I want my faith-life to show in my actions. I want my actions to be those of a woman who knows that all my struggles can be considered the ingredients of joy. Today, no matter what hard things come at me, I will stay focused on what you are doing in my life. In the name of Jesus, amen.

Looking for Joy
in All the Wrong Places

This is what the Almighty LORD, the Holy One of Israel, says: You can be saved by returning to me. You can have rest. You can be strong by being quiet and by trusting me. But you don't want that.

—Isaiah 30:15 GW

*I*f you're at all like me, you want to experience joy on a daily basis, but you're still not sure how to get there.

Let's return to our definition of joy. To experience joy every day, we have to start with a definition that isn't about happy feelings but about assurance that God is in control of the details of our lives. It's about developing confidence that, because he is in control, ultimately everything will be okay. And it is a moment-by-moment deliberate decision to choose joy no matter what.

Even though the Bible tells us joy is available to all of us, it eludes many, including me. In desperation, we try anything and everything we think might hold out the possibility of quenching our thirst for joy. And have you noticed how ridiculously easy it is to look for joy in all the wrong places? Our frantic search often leads us astray. Let's look at some of the typical ways we try to find joy.

People

Even though we know better, almost every day we expect the people around us to bring us joy—to meet our needs, take care of us, make us happy, understand us, and appreciate us. We expect them to love us perfectly all of the time! And when they don't—or can't—we get mad or hurt or feel betrayed and abandoned. It's incredibly challenging to feel joyful when the people closest to us let us down or disappoint us—especially if we look to them as the main source of our joy. I hate to tell you this, but people will fail you on a regular basis.

Possessions

We often allow our material belongings—or lack of them—to shape our joy. A new pair of shoes, a night on the town, a new computer program, a better car, all have the power to improve our mood and outlook. They don't call it retail "therapy" for nothing! But at best, possessions are a momentary distraction—they just don't lead to joy.

Places

For many of us, we've allowed where we live to be the key to our sense of fulfillment and joy. Which side of town, which side of the street, which side of the tracks, what city, what state, what country, what neighborhood, what view, what shape our house is in, what our yard looks like—these are powerful drivers in our search for joy. And yet, somehow when we arrive at the new home, the new state, the new neighborhood—it's never enough.

Positions

Where do we fit on the totem pole at work? Are we climbing up the ladder fast enough? Who's ahead of us? Who do we need to knock down so we can advance? More importantly, who's behind us? Who's sneaking up, waiting for the moment to knock us off our perch? We spend a lot of time looking to where we are in the hierarchy of our family, work, or community to find our joy, and for many, this can make or break our level of contentment.

Do you know what these four sources of joy have in common? They're all false. They all disappoint and fail to satisfy the deepest longing for joy in our souls. That's why the Bible says in Matthew 6:19–21 (NLT):

Don't store up treasures here on earth, where moths eat them and rust destroys them, and where thieves break in and steal. Store your treasures in heaven, where moths and rust cannot destroy, and thieves do not break in and steal. Wherever your treasure is, there the desires of your heart will also be.

People, possessions, places, and positions are just too flimsy to hold up the weight of our expectations and quench our thirst for joy.

Will you pray with me?

Father, you know I have looked to people, possessions, places, and positions for lasting joy. Forgive me for forsaking you, the true source of my joy. Help me to turn to you first for satisfaction. In the name of Jesus, amen.

If Only

Always be full of joy in the Lord. I say it again—
rejoice!

—Philippians 4:4 NLT

There's one more false source with which we try to quench our thirst for joy—our personality.

Joy doesn't come naturally to my personality—I've struggled with low-level depression for as long as I can remember. So it's been easy for me to conclude that joy is simply not available to someone like me. It's tempting for those of us who struggle with depression and discouragement to just forget about it and let the slappy happy people own joy.

There's an abundance of material on personality and personality types and how they affect us—but I like things simpler. I've reduced all I've heard about personality types down to four categories, using a whimsical approach: the Winnie-the-Pooh School of Personalities.

Tiggers

Tiggers are bouncy, flouncy, trouncy, pouncy, fun, fun, fun, fun, fun! These are the people who bound through life with a spring in their step. They laugh loudly (I've decided they do everything loudly) at parties, they tell jokes, and they think everyone is their best friend— even if they can't remember your name. Of course joy comes easily to them, right?

Winnie-the-Poohs

These gentle folks never get too excited about anything, but they usually have a pleasant look on their faces. They tend to have a hard time making up their minds about anything and are usually happy to let someone else make the decisions. You ask them about going to lunch: "Oh, you decide." You say: "No, it's your turn to choose." They say: "Oh no, please, you decide!" You try again: "Come on, I'd like to go where you'd like to go." They aren't giving in: "No, really, you choose." Finally, through clenched teeth, you agree to make the decision: "Fine! I'll choose!" Their joy might not be as easily apparent as a Tigger's, but surely they experience it, right?

Rabbits

Rabbits are the taskmasters of this world. Their motto is "Get it done, get it done right, and get it done now!" Rabbits have a to-do list the size of Montana and they don't let much get in their way. They're usually not the people you want to talk to if you're having a rough day, because they're likely to tell you to "just deal with it." Sometimes I wonder if Rabbits can experience much joy, and suspect that if they do, it's usually because they got to check something off their to-do list!

Eeyores

These are my favorite, because I understand Eeyores. I am one! Eeyores are intense, serious people—they even have their own personal little rain cloud over their heads all the time. They feel things deeply, and express things deeply, and get quite annoyed at all those stupid Tiggers who won't stop smiling! And yes, joy seems pretty elusive for the Eeyores of this world.

It's easy to look at people with other personalities and think, *I could be joyful if I were like them. Of course I could.* But that's not what Scripture teaches us. Joy is for everyone— Tiggers, Winnie-the-Poohs, Rabbits, and even gloomy old Eeyores. Joy is our birthright from the Holy Spirit and comes from being connected to God.

Galatians 5:22–23 tells us that the fruit of the Holy Spirit is "love, joy, peace, forbearance, kindness, goodness, faithfulness, gentleness and self-control." It doesn't say that joy is available to those whose natural personality lends itself easily to feelings of joy. No! It implies that it is available for everyone—all who are in Christ Jesus, those whose lives are full of the Holy Spirit.

Our human personalities don't limit our ability to experience joy. True joy is a gift of the Holy Spirit intended for all personalities at all times. That gives me hope. That leads me to the foundational truth we all need to remember: God is the only true source of joy.

Will you pray with me?

Father, thank you. Thank you that my personality does not dictate my ability to choose joy. Thank you for the gift of joy, my birthright as your child. Thank you for being my only true and reliable source of joy, no matter what happens. In the name of Jesus, amen.

Dry Wells

> My people have committed two sins: They
> have forsaken me, the spring of living water,
> and have dug their own cisterns, broken cis-
> terns that cannot hold water.
>
> —Jeremiah 2:13

We've talked about our search to find joy in people, possessions, places, position, and our personality. Five false sources of joy we typically look to as we try to experience joy. But the key word is *false*. These five sources of joy aren't really sources at all . . . they just appear to be. So if they're fake, why do we keep going back to them? Why don't we figure it out?

We can find the answer in Jeremiah 2:13: "My people have committed two sins: They have forsaken me, the spring of living water, and have dug their own cisterns, broken cisterns that cannot hold water."

Anyone not raised on a farm or a ranch might not know what a cistern is—it's just an underground container to catch and hold water.

When Jeremiah delivered the message of God in Jeremiah 2:13, the nation of Israel was in exile, far from God because they had worshipped other idols and rebelled against him. In this verse, God mentions two of the specific ways Israel had disobeyed him: they had forsaken him, the spring of living water, and then, to add insult to injury, they were trying to satisfy their thirst by themselves.

The Bible is a long record of the Israelites encountering God, the spring of living water who could quench their deepest thirst—literally and figuratively. And yet repeatedly they acknowledged that he was the true God but chose to ignore him, walk away from him, and flaunt their rebellion.

Larry Crabb's excellent book *Inside Out* was a great help in my understanding of this passage in Jeremiah. With his insights, I've come to picture their experience like this: it's as though they are hopelessly lost in the desert, dying of thirst, seeking anything to quench their parched, dry throats. They see a kiosk ahead with big flashing neon lights, and God is holding up a sign that says "Living Water Available Here." They see the kiosk and the lights. They see the sign that promises relief. They see God . . . and yet inexplicably they say, "No thanks, God! We appreciate your offer, but we see a shovel over there. We'll just dig our own cisterns!" Over and over they abandoned God, who had not just water but a spring of water—a source that would never dry up. They decided to figure it out by themselves. But Israel discovered that the cisterns they dug were broken—they couldn't hold water and they remained "thirsty" for God.

I can identify with the dry-as-a-bone Israelites.

On more than one occasion, I've had a really rough day—any number of things have gone wrong. I've felt down and a little discouraged. What I have done so many times is to feel the emptiness and ache in my soul—and decide to call a friend! "I'll call so and so; she always makes me feel better! Or I'll call my husband. He cheers me up!" And maybe I do just that, and I find myself feeling a little bit better. But shortly, I realize the good feelings are gone, and I'm still lonely or afraid or upset. So then I decide I'll feel better if I turn on the TV—you know, distract myself. And it works. For a while. But the bad feelings are still there. As I walk through the kitchen, the refrigerator calls my name and I think to myself, *That's it! Food will make it better!* And so I consume mass quantities of chips and salsa and guacamole and last night's roast with potatoes and carrots . . . hmmm . . . still empty. Chocolate! Chocolate fixes everything. So after eating my approved one ounce of dark chocolate, I take stock of where I'm at: I've talked to a friend, distracted myself from my worries, I've eaten far too much—and I'm still sad inside. I shouldn't be surprised, nor should you. Attempting to make our thirst disappear by digging our own cisterns will never satisfy. They're broken and cannot hold water.

What God desires for us to do when our thirst is intense is to immediately seek him, the spring of living water. He wants us to read his Word and remind ourselves of his ability to quench the ache in our soul. He asks that we meditate on his love and his power, maybe even listen to some music that reinforces our faith in him. Most of all, he gently reminds us that those five sources of joy we cling to are false and will *always* let us down.

One more thing. Like the rebellious Israelites, we add insult to injury. We have the nerve to expect God to help us dig our own cisterns! We get angry when it seems like he won't help us feel better, feel more joy. We're shoveling dirt as fast as we can and nothing gets any better. We bitterly accuse him of not caring. My friends, God will never help us dig our own cisterns. He will never help us seek joy outside of himself.

Will you pray with me?

God, I am not very good at this. I keep trying to be my own source of joy, when you offer a never-ending supply to anyone who asks. Forgive me. Thank you for leading me back to yourself. In the name of Jesus, amen.

The Source of Joy

There I will go to the altar of God—to God, the source of all my joy.

—Psalm 43:4 NLT

If you're like me, you've made some pretty serious attempts at digging your own cisterns, trying to secure your own source of joy. We've all done it, more times than we can count. We've all expected people, possessions, places, positions, and personalities to give us joy. And doing so has left us exhausted to the point of despair. I don't know about you, but I'm tired of being thirsty all the time. I'm tired of seeking joy in places where it can't be found.

I want something more. I want to experience something that lasts. The good news is that what God offers lasts.

What God offers is himself. *He* is the true source of joy. Say it with me: "God is the true source of joy."

We should probably repeat it over and over and over like a litany or a prayer, until it becomes embedded in our minds.

We have the assurance of the Word on this. Nehemiah 8:10 says, "The joy of the Lord is your strength." Isaiah 58:14 says, "Then you will find your joy in the Lord." And Psalm 16:11 says, "You will fill me with joy in Your presence."

These verses make it clear where joy is to be found and who is its author; joy is found in God because he is its source.

If we are going to experience joy on a daily basis, we need some changes to take place on the inside—not with how we feel but with how we think. We usually put the cart before the horse on this. We are convinced that we need to feel differently without realizing that how we feel is determined by what we think. It is our thinking that must change first, and then different feelings will eventually follow.

We must develop some convictions in our mind. God's truths have to become cemented and solid so that they begin to affect our feelings and our actions. That's what creates a settled assurance about God. And the more we know and understand God, the more easily we recognize that the words of Nehemiah are true: the joy of the Lord is our strength.

Here's one truth to start with: there is always something to praise God for.

During some moments in our lives it seems as though everything is in upheaval, and the blessings appear to have dried up. It seems like God has forgotten about us and those we love and that there are no more miracles to be had. But that isn't true. God hasn't changed; he remains constant, the same God he has always been. He was faithful before, he'll be faithful again.

But how do we remember that in the hard times—when the train track of sorrow seems much larger than the train track of joy? The secret is in learning how to meditate on who God is. Meditation doesn't mean to put your mind in neutral and mindlessly sit and breathe. Meditating on God is active; the word *meditate* means to contemplate, ponder, think, consider, and reflect. When we're meditating on God, we're putting our brains to work. Saint Padre Pio stated, "Through the study of books one seeks God; by meditation one finds him."

Here's another truth: *God never changes.* Everything else around you may change, but he does not. He will be there when the person you love is gone. He will be there when the possessions get lost. He will be there when the place you live is so unsatisfying. He will be there when the position is given to someone else. He will be there when you look at yourself and wish you were someone else. He will always be God. And that is always a reason for joy!

Will you pray with me?
God, I'd like to know you better. I'd like to learn to saturate my mind with your

truth so that I will come to know you as the only source of my joy. Thank you for your unchanging nature and your Word, and help me meditate on both today. In the name of Jesus, amen.

Praising God
for Who He Is

Our help is in the name of the LORD, the maker
of heaven and earth.

—Psalm 124:8 GW

*J*oy seems easy to find on the good days.
But when the blessings dry up, what do
we do? How do we praise God when circumstances leave us little to be grateful for? How
do we find joy in the middle of problems? Re-
membering the truth that God never changes,
and praising him for who he is rather than
for what he has given, will give us an endless

supply of things to praise him for. You and I can meditate on God's *worth*, his *will*, his *word*, his *works*, and his *ways*. Let's dive into a couple of these today.

God's Worth Is Incomparable

What does *worth* mean? Worth refers to the qualities that command respect, honor, and esteem. What can we learn about God's name or his nature that commands respect, honor, or esteem?

Let's start with Psalm 148:13: "Let them praise the name of God. It's the only Name worth praising. His radiance exceeds anything on earth and sky" (MSG).

In this verse we learn God's name is the only name worth praising. That gives me pause—because I can think of a boatload of people in the news who think they are worthy of praise. Does that mean, then, that we don't praise other people—only God? No. But God is special because his radiance exceeds anything on earth or sky. It means God is different than any human being, and as such, he is worthy of my praise.

A few years ago I could not find a peaceful, joyful place within me. Since I live near the Pacific Ocean, many times after dropping my kids off at school I would drive to the beach and park on a cliff above the ocean. I remember one day in particular feeling very hopeless— but staring out at that vast sea, I felt comfort. The God who created those waters was bigger and grander than any created thing. If he could command the universe, he was surely big enough to handle what was breaking my heart. The words of 1 Chronicles 16:25—"Great is the Lord and most worthy of praise"—became my reality in those moments.

When we start to catch a glimpse of who God really is and remember his incomparable worth, it begins to restore our joy.

God's Will Is Good

Many times in our lives we feel as if we're flying blind. Circumstances have left us confused and unsure. In our panic we cry out to God, reminding him how dark it is, how hard it is to see what's next in our lives. It is in those kinds of moments we can turn to Jeremiah 29:11, which tells us, "'For I know the plans I have for you,' declares the Lord, 'plans to prosper you and not to harm you, plans to give you hope and a future.'"

There's so much to ponder and reflect on in this verse. Contrary to what many of us believe, God's will *is* good . . . and his plans are not to harm us but to give us hope and a future. Let's take this phrase and think about it for a couple of days. Let's think about God's plan to prosper us, not to harm us. Let's think about his plans to give us a hope and a future. I believe meditating on the good will of God will fill us with joy. We will be reassured that God is for us, not against us—and when we are confident of that, we can face any trial with a sense of purpose.

As it says in Romans 8:31, "If God is for us, who can be against us?" This gives us a reason to be joyful today!

Will you pray with me?

Father, I praise you, the name above all names. I thank you for the joy you offer because of who you are, no matter what my life circumstances are. Your worth is incomparable, and your will for me is good. I am grateful. In the name of Jesus, amen.

God's Word Is Reliable

The precepts of the LORD are right, giving joy
to the heart. The commands of the LORD are
radiant, giving light to the eyes.

—Psalm 19:8

The best part of meditating on who God is? We get to know him more intimately. Meditating is an energetic, intentional way of thinking, reflecting, and pondering, and it's aimed at knowing God. And when the trials and circumstances of your life cause you to doubt him, you will find you have grown to know him so intimately that you won't lose your hold on joy.

We talked about God's *worth*—that he is above all gods and deserving of our deepest praise. We talked about his *will*—that it is good and God can be trusted. Another attribute of God to meditate on is his *Word*; his Word is reliable. Psalm 19:8 in the Message calls God's Word a "life-map": "The life-maps of God are right, showing the way to joy."

I like that image. The Word of God is a stable, reliable life-map of truth for our everyday lives. Nothing else you read or watch can make that claim!

Truth, in our world, seems to be in the eye of the beholder. Because Rick and I have been in the media a lot in the last few years, I've had the opportunity up close and personal to see just how mixed up a story can get! It seems like no matter how careful we are to give a reporter or an interviewer the correct facts, somehow it gets tweaked and the details are wrong. That has made me cynical about every story or news report I read, because I know that it is never completely accurate. But the Bible isn't like that—it is completely accurate, reliable, and trustworthy. Knowing that, I can be assured that when I read God's Word, I'm getting the truth—a foundation I can build my life on. And having a sure foundation for my life leads to joy.

And the Bible is not just reliable—the Bible brings us joy. In Psalm 119:111 we read, "Your statutes are my heritage forever; they are the joy of my heart." Can you honestly say that about God's Word? Is what he says the joy of your heart? Maybe you're new to reading the Bible and a lot of it doesn't make sense to you yet, or you haven't quite wrapped your mind around it all. That's okay. It takes time; it takes meditation on what you read and time to think and contemplate how it might apply to your life. Becoming comfortable with being a Christ-follower and comfortable with God's Word is sort of like learning about a different culture than the one you were raised in. At first the language seems hard to understand, the cultural customs seem a bit odd, and you're never quite sure if you're doing the right thing at the right moment! But eventually, it starts to make sense to you; not only does it makes sense, it brings great joy!

The prophet Jeremiah responded to God's words in a rather unorthodox fashion—he actually ate them to vividly make a point to the nation of Israel. Jeremiah 15:16 says, "When your words came, I ate them; they were my joy and my heart's delight." By his action he was saying, "God's words are so tasty and satisfying to my soul that I *ate* them!" Don't worry—that doesn't mean God wants us all to *eat* his word. But he will ask you to meditate on it, to get to know him better and better through his word so that your confidence in him won't be shaken by circumstances that seem out of your control. And like Jeremiah, you just might say, "Your word is my joy and my heart's delight."

Will you pray with me?

God, may I respond to your Word with joy, each and every day. May I read it knowing the love you have for me and the great gift of your joyful presence within its pages. In the name of Jesus, amen.

God's Works
Are Awesome

God's works are so great, worth a lifetime of
study—endless enjoyment!

—Psalm 111:2 MSG

As we seek to get to know God better, I
want to suggest that you spend some
time today meditating on God's works, because
they are *awesome*!

His "works" are the things he has created—
the world and all that fills it. The trees, the
flowers, the mountains, the clouds, the sky,
the sun, the animals that populate the earth,

the bugs, the ocean, the fish in the ocean, the stars, the planets, the wind, the snow—*all* of it made by his loving, creative, awesome power. What he has made is so great we could actually spend an entire lifetime studying it, and in so doing, we experience endless enjoyment . . . joy.

You may not all live near an amazing ocean or pristine forest. But we can all stare at a tree fluttering in the breeze for a while. We can spend a few minutes studying the intricacies of a blackberry. We can watch an ant on the driveway carry a huge piece of grass back home.

In 1 Chronicles 16:33 we read, "Let the trees of the forest sing, let them sing for joy before the LORD." This verse says God's works actually sing to him! I can't hear it, but God can. I often wonder if it's sort of like how only dogs can hear a dog whistle. You and I can't hear it, but dogs start putting their paws over their ears because it is a tone their ears can pick up. Maybe the trees and the bushes and the oceans and the mountains and the clouds are singing every day and I just can't hear them! And if they sing, why don't we?

Honestly? Probably because sometimes I'm just having a rotten day. My hair didn't curl the way I wanted it to, or the price of gasoline rose again, or it's raining—or grief has knocked me to the floor again. The reasons vary from the mundane to the profound. I explain, all too easily, to him, "I'm down today, God—I can't sing. I simply cannot praise you right now."

All of God's creation praises and sings to him except one: people. Why do I hold back my songs of praise for trivialities? Why do I hold back my songs of praise in the pain? His works, his creation, sing for joy before him. And when I meditate on what he has made, on his stunning abilities as the master Creator, I want to sing . . . I too want to shout for joy.

So today—will you sing? Psalm 92:4 says, "For you make me glad by your deeds, LORD. I sing for joy at what your hands have done." Will you study what he has made—will you be amazed at his works and praise him? You can choose to do so, no matter what kind of day you're having. No matter what your feelings tell you, no matter what mood you're in, you

can make a choice to rejoice today. You don't
have to have a great voice to sing praises—you
can croak like a toad or bark like a dog. Any
joyful noise will be sufficient. He doesn't care
about your vocal ability or even what song you
sing, but he does care about your heart's ability to enter into praise for who he is and what
he has made.

Will you pray with me?

*Here we are, God—to tell you that
you are worthy, that you are reliable, and
that we trust you. Today we are choosing
to lift our voices in praise to you. In the
name of Jesus, a man of joy, amen.*

God's Ways Are Loving

You protect me with salvation-armor; you
hold me up with a firm hand, caress me with
your gentle ways.

—Psalm 18:35 MSG

Why is it so important to explore ways to
meditate on God and to get to know
him better? Because as human beings, we have
a nasty tendency to turn on God when things
don't go our way. We often shake our fists in
his face and say, "What have you done for me
lately, God? I know you've shown up in the
past, but what about today? I need help *now*!"
And if we feel like he doesn't give us the answer

we are desperately seeking, or if our situation doesn't improve, we start to get angry or fearful and begin to accuse him of not caring for us.

We can get a better handle on this very human tendency by learning how to meditate on God's *ways*—because God's ways are loving.

There have been a number of times when I haven't felt like God's hands on my life were gentle or tender, as Psalm 18:35 reminds me; rather, those hands felt very heavy. I have felt like I was going to cave in with the weight of the burdens I was carrying. Of course, those are the moments when Satan jumps in with his own suggestions: doubt God, stop believing that God is good or loving, give up and walk away from him. Those are the moments in which knowing and believing in the ways of God that we read about in God's Word are critical. That's when I go back to the Bible and read verses like these two:

> His love has taken over our lives. God's faithful ways are eternal. Hallelujah!
>
> Psalm 117:2 (MSG)

The Lord is trustworthy in all he promises
and faithful in all he does.

Psalm 145:13

We've all had at least one moment in which
we said, "God, you couldn't be a loving God and
allow *this* to happen to me." But his Word—
which is reliable—says he is loving toward all he
has made. I can choose to believe and trust that
God's ways are loving whether I can see it or not.

For me, airplane travel is a perfect situation
in which to practice this. I hate to fly. What I
dislike most is when I open that little plastic
window shade, only to see nothing but gray
mist. I start to panic inside and think if I can't
see what's out there, the pilot must not be able
to either, which means we're going down! The
same thing happens in my relationship with
God. There are dark and scary times when I
look at what is happening and say, "God, I can't
see! And if I can't see, that must mean you can't
see; and if you can't see, I'm definitely going
down." Faith in God often means trusting God
when life is a gray mist—and I hate it. I hate the

sense of losing control and feeling powerless to change anything.

In these moments, we all need to remember that on a cloudy day, the sun is shining just as brightly as it did yesterday. We just can't see it. Just because I can't see what's next, or I can't explain why his hand seems heavy on my life, or the train track of sorrow just won't leave me or my family alone, doesn't mean that God isn't still in control. He is. And his ways are loving toward all he has made; that includes me and that includes you.

So take a deep breath, let it out—and spend some time today pondering our God's loving ways. He won't leave you or abandon you to face it all by yourself. He is with you—and his joy comes with him.

Will you pray with me?

Father, without you I would certainly perish. Forgive me for my fear when I can't see what the future holds. I know your ways are loving and you are in control of my life. Today I place my trust in you and choose joy. Amen.

Heaven's Value System

We know that God causes everything to work
together for the good of those who love God.

—Romans 8:28 NLT

Can meditating on God's worth, his will,
his word, his works, and his ways change
us? And how does meditation increase our joy?
Those are great questions.

Meditating on the truths about God changes
our value system. When we start believing the
truths about God and repeat them to ourselves
over and over—things that are very hard to say,
like, "Your ways are loving. Your will is good
even when I can't see it or understand it"—our

value system begins to change. It may take some time, but we start to value the things God values, and what was important before begins to matter less. And when our value system shifts to that of heaven's, joy takes root and blossoms in our lives. When I value what God values, I begin to find joy in the only place where it can truly be found.

What is God's value system? God values character over comfort, faith over fear, mercy over judgment, justice over injustice, people over possessions, truth over falsehood, humility over pride, hope over despair, love over apathy. In other words, God values the things that will last; he has an eternal perspective. And he invites us to view life from that same perspective, to believe that he is at work in history and in our personal story in ways that often remain mysterious to us. Whether we see it or not, he is redeeming what has been stolen and healing what has been broken—every night, every day.

In Romans 8:28 we read, "We know that God causes everything to work together for the good of those who love God" (NLT). So we can be joyful at all times—not because everything in our lives is good or pleasant or right. Joy is not based on outward circumstances but on inward certainties. If we are certain that he is working behind the scenes to fit all the details of our lives into his good plans, then we can develop the quiet confidence that ultimately everything is going to be all right. That's not the equivalent of saying "Don't worry, be happy" or some other nifty little phrase. Believing that ultimately everything is going to be all right takes into account loved ones dying, financial loss, hopes dashed, dreams not realized. Choosing to believe that he is always working, knitting together the fragments of our lives, always in control of it all, means that it will work together for my good and his glory.

Of course, it would be great if God would just provide all the answers now—this very moment! And we want more than simple answers. We want explanations in triplicate with a certification that God is qualified to make those decisions. That's why the word *ultimately* is in our definition of joy. He doesn't promise answers or explanations on demand—he's not like our DVR, where we call up a movie at the click of a button. God's working out of all things for our good rests on the truth that Oswald Chambers discovered: "I know now, God, why you utter no answers, you yourself are the answer. In your presence, all questions fade away."

Ultimately we will know. But what I know today is this: choosing the eternal over the temporary leads to joy.

Will you pray with me?

Lord, teach me how to align my value system with yours. Help me choose the eternal over the temporary. Build in me the settled assurance that you are in control, and a quiet confidence that ultimately everything will be all right because you are God. In the name of Jesus Christ, amen.

Do Not Lose Heart

So we fix our eyes not on what is seen, but on what is unseen, since what is seen is temporary, but what is unseen is eternal.

—2 Corinthians 4:18

When I get to heaven, of course I'm going to make a mad dash to see Jesus and spend a few thousand years talking to him. But the next person I want to see and talk to is the apostle Paul. He blows me away. He is such a hero of the faith, such an example and model of how to live a godly, joy-filled life in spite of terrible opposition and struggle. Nobody knew better than Paul that joy is not based on outward circumstances but on inward certainties. The Bible records part of Paul's story in 2 Corinthians 11. He was unjustly imprisoned, whipped, beaten, stoned, shipwrecked, in danger from bandits, rivers, seas, and false believers, hungry, thirsty, cold, and naked. And yet he had the audacity to say this:

- Rejoice in the Lord always. (Phil 4:4, NIV)
- In everything give thanks. (1 Thes 5:18, KJV)
- I can do all things through Christ who strengthens me. (Phil 4:13, NKJV)
- Be joyful in hope, patient in affliction, faithful in prayer. (Romans 12:12, NIV)
- I have learned the secret of being content in any and every situation (Phil 4:12, NIV)
- We rejoice in our sufferings. (Romans 5:3, ESV)

How could he respond like that? How could he have that kind of attitude after suffering so much? Many of those statements were made while he was in prison, chained to a Roman guard! How did he do it?

He was able to say those statements and believe in their truth because he had aligned his values with the value system of heaven; he chose the eternal over the temporary time and time again. Although he was in chains on the outside, on the inside he was free. And as long as you and I are tied to the world's value system of seeking joy in people, possessions, places, position, and personalities, we will never find joy. It is only in choosing the eternal over the temporary that we find freedom—and joy.

If you had asked Paul if he was comfortable in a prison cell, he would probably have said no. He wasn't a machine or a robot or a zombie. He was a man who missed his friends, who would have loved to have a couple warm blankets, and who would much rather have been out traipsing around the Roman Empire talking about Jesus than be cooped up in prison, chained to a guard. But in the end, his circumstances didn't matter as much as the work that God was accomplishing through his sufferings.

In 2 Corinthians 4:16–18 Paul encourages both us and himself: "Therefore we do not lose heart. Though outwardly we are wasting away, yet inwardly we are being renewed day by day. For our light and momentary troubles are achieving for us an eternal glory that far outweighs them all. So we fix our eyes not on what is seen, but on what is unseen, since what is seen is temporary, but what is unseen is eternal."

Paul had learned long before that God was the only true source of joy. He had already experienced the pain of friends who abandoned him, cities that closed their doors to him, earthly possessions that couldn't satisfy, education that couldn't save him, and a personality that often got him into trouble. God was Paul's only true source of joy, and because of that, he consistently, faithfully chose to focus not on what he could see with his eyes but on what he could see with his spirit.

No wonder he could urge us two thousand years later to rejoice, to give thanks in everything, to be content with what we have, to be patient in affliction, and to not lose heart.

Heaven's value system was his and so were heaven's joys.

Will you pray with me?

God, I want to rejoice in all things, to be content, to not lose heart. I want to understand with my whole heart what Paul knew, that you are the only true source of joy. I need your help and depend on your grace today. In the name of Jesus, amen.

A Faith That Shines

These trials will show that your faith is genuine. It is being tested as fire tests and purifies gold—though your faith is far more precious than mere gold.

—1 Peter 1:7 NLT

e've spent a good amount of time together identifying false sources of joy that we all turn to at one point or another, and zeroing in on the only true source of joy—God himself. We've talked about how joy starts with a conviction of our minds—coming to the realization that while everything around us is shaky and unpredictable, God remains stable and true and worthy of our praise, even when we don't like what is happening to us.

But joy is more than a state of mind. It also involves the condition of our *hearts* and is reflected in our attitudes and emotions—especially when times get rocky.

We read in James 1 that troubles expose our faith-life. When troubles come, the curtain of our faith is drawn back and we see what has been hiding behind the veil—and it's not always a pretty picture. We see all the weakness, the failure, the instability of our commitment to Christ. We suddenly get a realistic look at how vibrant our faith really is, or isn't. And when troubles come, we can't fool ourselves any longer into thinking we're deep and strong and full of faith if we're not. Circumstances will always reveal the true nature of our walk with God, and often it's just not as great as we thought it was.

And it's not just us who can see our faith-life for what it really is. Philippians 2:14–15 tells us, "In everything you do, stay away from complaining and arguing so that no one can speak a word of blame against you. You are to live clean, innocent lives as children of God in a dark world full of people who are crooked and stubborn. Shine out among them like beacon lights" (TLB).

Not only is my faith-life on display for me to evaluate myself, but I'm on display to a watching world! Everyone—non-Christian or Christian—has struggles; we go through the same types of problems. But Paul says that the difference between the way a Christian and a non-Christian face troubles should be so stark and distinct that we will shine like stars in a dark night. The contrast should be amazing and unmistakable. A watching world wants to know "How *does* a Christ-follower respond when the bottom falls out?" I want them to see something that gives hope and leads them to trust God themselves; I want my faith-life on display to reveal courage and strength and audacious faith in the face of dead-end situations.

Often the world thinks God is a big joke. Why? Because of us—because often we're a big joke. They notice that we talk a good game but have an extremely difficult time living out what we say we believe. They take notes and decide God must not be big enough or powerful enough to get us through the rough spots, because we act just like them. Why should they rely on God when we don't? Instead of shining stars that point to an all-powerful, all-loving God, we blend into the darkness.

But the "world" is not my only audience. I want my children and grandchildren to see something new and different. I don't want them to see a woman shredded by her pain but instead a woman who, through her tears, still clings passionately to God; a woman who hasn't lost faith in the God of miracles; a woman who has confidence to hope for the future; and a woman who chooses joy in the present, no matter how much she is surrounded by trouble. I want Jesus, the man of joy, to be seen in me.

Today, as we live with the knowledge that our faith-life is on display for all to see, may our responses to trouble point to Jesus and to joy.

Will you pray with me?

Father, I struggle when troubles expose my faith-life; I'm not sure I really want my family, friends, or co-workers to know all the ways I stumble. Help me to focus not on the ways I fail to shine but on your delight in me. Help me to draw close to you so I can build a stronger faith-life that includes joy in all things. In Jesus's name, amen.

Finding Grace

Even before he made the world, God loved us
and chose us in Christ to be holy and without
fault in his eyes.

—Ephesians 1:4 NLT

As I seek to discover how to live a joyful life, I've made a pretty horrendous discovery about myself, and I'll bet it's true of many of you as well. As much as I *say* I want to become more joyful, I actively sabotage joy in myself and in others. Instead of cultivating heart responses that allow me to shine like a star in a dark night, I work overtime at beating down any little hints of joy that might start to blossom!

I don't want to do that anymore. Instead of being a joy-killer, I want to be a joy-builder. I want to fill myself with joy and fill others' lives with joy. So how can we all cultivate a heart response that allows joy to build inside of us?

We begin by focusing on grace rather than keeping rules.

For those of you for whom a rule is nothing more than something to be broken, this may sound like a piece of cake. But this is really hard for me, a dyed-in-the-wool rule-follower. I love rules! Rules keep me safe, they make life manageable, and they provide a pathway in every situation. Let me clarify—I like the rules *I* make, not necessarily the ones others make. My rules make sense; yours probably don't. What a hypocrite I can be!

For people like me, God offers the entire book of Galatians to teach that rules in and of themselves cannot give life . . . or joy.

Galatians 3:12 reminds us, "Rule keeping does not naturally evolve into living by faith, but only perpetuates itself in more and more rule keeping" (MSG).

And we read in Galatians 3:21, "For if any kind of rule-keeping had power to create life in us, we would certainly have gotten it by this time" (MSG).

I lived most of my young adult life as a Christian desperately trying to keep all the rules. Although I didn't say it aloud, in my heart I was convinced that God would bless me more . . . love me more . . . if I kept all the rules. The problem is that every group of believers has their own interpretation of what the rules are, and I found myself weary, frustrated, and disappointed in my ability to do it all "right." I didn't understand grace.

Grace is the face God wears when he meets my sin, my weakness, and my imperfection. And grace is possible because of what Jesus did for me and you. In Ephesians 1:4 we read, "For he chose us *in him* before the creation of the world to be holy and blameless in his sight" (emphasis mine).

When we became Christians, God placed us "in Christ," and we are now completely acceptable to him. This concept is very important; God wants to make sure we understand that rule-keeping isn't the key to our relationship with him—being "in Christ" is.

Here's an exercise to help us see what the life of grace—life "in Christ"—looks like. Find a small piece of paper. This represents you. It can be torn, dirty, or marked up—it doesn't matter. Now place that paper within the pages of a book and close it tightly. Turn the book over in your hands; that paper is "in" the book, and if you didn't know any better, you wouldn't have a clue it was there.

This is what God did for us. He took us and put us "in" Jesus Christ. When God looks at us, from any angle, all he can see is the perfection of his Son, Jesus. Today, and every day, we can leave the rule-keeping behind and find grace.

Will you pray with me?

Father, today I want to build joy. Help me to turn from my joy-stealing habits and give thanks that you have placed me in Christ, fully accepted and redeemed. In the name of your Son, amen.

Trusting God
for the Future

Give all your worries and cares to God, for
he cares about you.

—1 Peter 5:7 NLT

By far the hardest of the Bible's commands for me to obey and live out are "Don't worry about anything" and "Rejoice always." It's not because I think they're wrong. I know the truth—nothing kills joy faster than worry! But we all worry, and some of us are really good at it. Some people just worry about their health; some just worry about their kids;

some just worry about finances. But some of us worry about absolutely everything! If there were jobs for professional worriers, some of us could earn money—we're that good at it!

It's impossible to be joyful and full of worry at the same time—they cancel each other out.

So if you're among the constant worriers, anxiety has you in its death grip. All that worry is choking out the joy in your life. Remember our definition of joy: it is the settled assurance that God is in control of all the details of my life, the quiet confidence that ultimately everything is going to be all right, and the determined choice to praise God in all things.

Our antidote to worry is trust. Trust that God is in control of all the details of our lives. Our trust leads to confidence that it will all be okay—not that everything will turn out the way *I* want it to, but that God is at work in the details. Trust will loosen that death grip of worry and allow joy to flow back into your life. As a friend of mine in high school said, "When you're worrying, you're not trusting, and when you're trusting, you're not worrying."

Matthew 6:33–34 reads, "Steep your life in God-reality, God-initiative, God-provisions. Don't worry about missing out. You'll find all your everyday human concerns will be met. Give your entire attention to what God is doing right now, and don't get worked up about what may or may not happen tomorrow. God will help you deal with whatever hard things come up when the time comes" (MSG).

Most of us don't really believe that—I know it's a struggle for me. If we did, we wouldn't have sleepless nights or that tension in our shoulders; we wouldn't snap at people without cause or work all hours of the day and night without rest. We wouldn't run through our worst-case scenarios about the future, thinking to ourselves, *What will happen when . . . ? How will I handle it if . . . ? What if she chooses to . . . ? What if he says . . . ?*

One of my favorite books is *The Hiding Place* by Corrie ten Boom. Corrie and her family hid Jews in a secret room in their house in the Netherlands during WWII. Eventually they were discovered, and Corrie and her family were imprisoned. Corrie tells the story of when she was a little girl, and she and her father would take the train to Amsterdam. She would always worry about where the ticket was. Her father would tell her, "Corrie, when we get to the train station, we will get the ticket. I will take care of it."

That's how God talks to us about our worries. "If or when that thing that frightens you happens, I will be there for you; I will take care of it. I will be enough."

I know how Corrie felt. A few years ago, a trip had me anxious. It got so bad that I was either going to have to cancel the trip or do something about it. So I turned to the Scriptures. I read of the angel Gabriel telling Mary, the mother of Jesus, that she was going to bear the Messiah. Though she must have been terrified of all the what-ifs, her response—immediately—was "I am the Lord's servant . . . May everything you have said about me come true" (Luke 1:38 NLT).

I realized I had inadvertently given my heart away to the lesser gods of fear and anxiety.

But trusting that God was in control of all the details of my life, even just for that moment, led to a profound peace.

Friends, bad things happen. This is earth, not heaven. I can't deny the reality of all that could go wrong and perhaps has already gone wrong. But as 1 Peter 5:7 says, we can throw the whole weight of our concerns upon God for *we* are his personal concern. We can find the peace that comes from trusting God; and when our hearts are at peace, joy returns.

Will you pray with me?

God, I don't know the future. I can't figure that out. But I believe you are enough for me today, and you will be enough for me tomorrow and the next day. Let my attitude be the same as Mary's. Let me come to a place of peace. In the name of Jesus, amen.

Finding Balance

It is no use for you to get up early and stay up late, working for a living. The Lord gives sleep to those he loves.

—Psalm 127:2 NCV

As we look for ways to build joy in ourselves, one of the traps all of us get caught in from time to time is overbooking our schedule. I have heard it said that "busyness fills a schedule but fractures a family." As true as that is, busyness will do more than fracture a family. It will kill joy.

We don't intentionally set out to live such frantic lives, but somehow before we know it, we are committed to too many tasks, too many responsibilities, too many obligations, and too many events. We find ourselves saying yes when we should say no and saying no when we should say yes.

As I fill my schedule, I've also discovered I'm a terrific liar. My ability to deceive myself is epic! I've told myself so many times, "This is only temporary; I won't live like this forever," only to find what was supposed to be temporary has become a way of life. Yes, there are unusual seasons of busyness, but it's far too easy to let a season become a pattern, a crisis mode to become the routine.

The Antidote? Balance

We know balance is tricky, but it's worth our attention and attempts. Achieving perfect balance is impossible; life is more like a river that ebbs and flows. We have moments where we spend more time on this priority, and then it shifts and we give another one of our priorities more attention. And yet when we stay connected to

Jesus, we are able to evaluate ourselves sanely and realistically.

You might need to spend some time asking yourself the hard questions about your work—and what it represents in your life. Why are you so driven? What does it say about you? What does it say about your relationship to God? What does it say about your view of yourself and your value as a person? What does busyness really represent in your life? I promise God will give you answers; you may not like what you hear, but he will give you insights if you honestly ask.

In Matthew 11:29–30 Jesus says, "Accept my work and learn from me. I am gentle and humble in spirit. And you will find rest for your souls. The work that I ask you to accept is easy. The load I give you to carry is not heavy" (ICB).

Either Jesus was a liar or we're missing something. The obvious answer is we're missing something. If Jesus promises us that the load he gives is manageable, yet the pace of our lives is wiping us out, leaving us with little space to experience joy, it's time to make a change. It's time to simplify, reevaluate our priorities, and be willing to examine what God has asked us to do—and what we've added to our to-do list all by ourselves. Let's do the hard work of change, instead of whining and complaining about our heavy burdens.

At the end of our lives, will we be pleased with the decisions we made about the time that was given to us? More importantly, will God be pleased? The key is to yield control of our brief span of time to him daily, keeping in mind that depth, not speed, is the truest measure of a balanced life. And in our balance, we make room for joy.

Will you pray with me?

Father, my time is in your hands. Ultimately you set the course and span of my days. I want my time to display, for all to see, a woman of joy, confident that God is in control. Help me to choose balance over busyness today. In Jesus's name, amen.

Practicing Acceptance

> But what happens when we live God's way?
> He brings gifts into our lives, much the same
> way that fruit appears in an orchard—things
> like affection for others, exuberance about
> life, serenity.
>
> —Galatians 5:22 MSG

*W*hen I read those words from Galatians,
I wish I could say it felt within my
grasp every day. Gifts that appear like fruit in
an orchard? It sounds so easy, so natural. And
I would love that—to feel those fruits of the
spirit so naturally, things like love, joy, peace,
and patience. But my secret sin—or not so

secret, I suppose, if you hang around me for very long—is that I'm a perfectionist. I have been known to actually say out loud, "Why is perfection so difficult?" Most people laugh at me for being naïve and stupid enough to verbalize that crazy thought. But as a lifelong card-carrying member of the Perfectionist's Club of America, I start every day expecting to find perfection. You can imagine how quickly my disappointment sets in.

Before I've even left the house, I encounter imperfection. My hair won't curl the way I want it to. I wash a shirt exactly the way the manufacturer suggests and it still shrinks. I walk through my house turning off lights that others have left on and muttering to myself, "Why can't they get it right?"

When I go to church on the weekend, I pick up a bulletin and immediately find a typo. Then I look up at the screen for the lyrics to the songs we're singing—another typo. I listen to Rick preach and maybe I'll hear him say something that mortifies me. Or I look at the way I'm taking notes and observe that my handwriting is sloping, the letters not sitting precisely on the lines provided. Before I know it, worship has become just one more place of frustration and annoyance instead of a place of connection with God and his people.

Yeah . . . pretty sad. Pretty messed up, and definitely joyless. I can't think of a better way to kill the joy in myself than to expect perfection.

I need to remember perfection isn't difficult; it's *impossible*! It's impossible because of what happened with Adam and Eve in Genesis 2. When they blew it for the rest of us by eating the forbidden fruit, God said the punishment would be that the world would live under a curse—making perfection not just difficult but completely unattainable.

Richard Carlson writes, "I've yet to meet an absolute perfectionist whose life was filled with inner peace. The need for perfection and the desire for inner tranquility conflict with each other."

But before you feel guilty for wanting perfection, let me give you some good news. It's not wrong to long for perfection—you and I were made for it! We were made for perfect relationships. We were made for perfect bodies. We were made to live forever. So the longing inside of us for perfection is not wrong. What's wrong is to expect it here and now, on this broken planet filled with broken people, broken bodies, broken minds, and broken circumstances.

The antidote? Acceptance . . . of this imperfect world, of imperfect me, of imperfect you. Accept that we live under a curse as we wait for the perfection that is promised to be restored to us in heaven. When God describes the new heaven and the new earth in Revelation 22:3, he details all the beauty and loveliness—the perfection—that will be there, and states, "No longer will there be any curse."

That means hair that curls properly every time, bulletins with no typos, and conversations that never go sour because of misunderstanding. It will mean bodies that don't get sick, minds that function as designed, and no more accidents, betrayals, disappointments. Without the curse, there will be no hurt and no pain.

Let's hold on, all of us dyed-in-the-wool perfectionists. Perfection is coming. Until then, let's practice acceptance of ourselves and others, and let go of the rigid, demanding expectations that rob us of joy.

Will you pray with me?

Father, it's overwhelming to see how I have allowed criticism and perfectionism to take root in my heart and crowd out joy. Go deep inside me and do your work. Change me so that I become a woman of joy. In Jesus's name I pray, amen.

Nurturing Joy in Others

A joyful heart is good medicine.

—Proverbs 17:22 GW

We don't intentionally set out to kill joy in our family and friends; it's usually subtler than that. Honestly, most of us are clueless about how to build joy in those around us and just as clueless about the ways we squash the delicate flower of joy in them.

For instance, have you ever considered how doubting someone's motive robs them of joy? Unfortunately, we've become a jaded, cynical group of people. We've gotten accustomed to news reports of famous athletes who confess to performance-enhancing drugs, politicians who lobby for family-friendly legislation while visiting prostitutes on the side, pastors who live double lives, and husbands or wives who promise to love us forever only to leave us.

On top of the lies and failures of others, we recognize that *we* are not always entirely truthful or forthcoming. And we believe that if we lie, others must be lying as well. The result is a cynical attitude that doubts everyone and everything, refusing to take anyone at face value. We decide we know what someone really *means*, no matter what they *say*. How many arguments have you gotten into because you thought you had the other person all figured out without really listening to them?

The antidote to cynicism is to believe the best about the other person.

In the Living Bible, 1 Corinthians 13:7 says, "If you love someone, you will always be loyal to him no matter what the cost. You will always believe in him, always expect the best of him, and always stand your ground in defending him." Can we do that today? Maybe it's time to let the past be the past and let somebody have a second chance or twenty-second chance. Maybe it's time to start believing the best instead of the worst.

Another way we can build joy in someone else is to offer nonjudgmental love instead of emphasizing their mistakes. If you're a perfectionist like me, you're probably someone who struggles with criticizing and judging others. I've been goofy enough to say, "Yes, I'm a perfectionist, but I just hold people to the same standards I hold myself." Yeah . . . right . . . and Santa Claus is coming in July this year.

But Luke 6:37 tells us, "Don't pick on people, jump on their failures, criticize their faults—unless, of course, you want the same treatment. Don't condemn those who are down; that hardness can boomerang. Be easy on people; you'll find life a lot easier" (MSG).

The fact is, I can't even meet my own standards, so there's no way you can measure up. Focusing on the imperfections in others destroys joy in them. We rationalize our judgmental tendencies by saying, "I thought you would want to know!" as though people should be grateful that we love them enough to point out their flaws.

We need to recognize our criticism of others has nothing to do with them but everything to do with our need to be critical. Read Romans 2:1 with me: "Every time you criticize someone, you condemn yourself. It takes one to know one. Judgmental criticism of others is a well-known way of escaping detection in your own crimes and misdemeanors" (MSG).

You and I have a choice: we can focus our attention on the 80 percent of another person that we love and admire or we can harp on the 20 percent we disapprove of. Which way do you think produces joy in others? Yep . . . choosing to find joy in the parts of them that are worthy of admiration and affirmation, minimizing the parts that need work. This brings joy not just to them but ourselves as well!

Will you pray with me?
Father, today, with your help, I will choose to build joy in others by believing

the best about them and offering love without judgment. In doing so, I know you offer me the chance to choose joy for myself as well. In the name of Jesus, amen.

Gifts of Compassion
and Appreciation

And become useful *and* helpful *and* kind to
one another, tenderhearted (compassionate,
understanding, loving-hearted), forgiving one
another (readily and freely) as God in Christ
forgave you.

—Ephesians 4:32 AMP

*B*uilding joy in ourselves and others
means we need to recognize what we
do that destroys joy. Here's one that can be
subtle—we minimize others' feelings.

I'm not sure where we get the idea that we
can successfully diagnose what another is truly

feeling. Usually we're very much out of touch with our own feelings and yet suddenly we're Dr. Phil when it comes to other people! We say things like, "What you *really* mean is. . . ." or "I know what you're *really* feeling." That's pretty arrogant! The truth is, we don't know. Proverbs 14:10 says, "Each heart knows its own bitterness, and no one else can fully share its joy" (NLT).

Instead of validating the other person's feelings, we often work overtime to point out how illogical their feelings are . . . how wrong they are . . . how they *should* be feeling. If somebody says "It's cold in here!" and we automatically say, "No, it's not." If a friend tells us, "I'm depressed" and we quickly jump in and tell them why there's no reason to be depressed. When they say, "I'm feeling pretty good about this situation," and we caution, "I don't think I would be if I were you." In short order, "different" becomes "wrong" or "false" or "illogical." Telling someone else their feelings aren't valid kills joy every time.

The solution to minimizing the feelings of others is compassion. And part of compassion is offering validation. Validation simply acknowledges what someone feels—letting them know you heard them. We all long for validation that our thoughts and feelings are heard and understood by someone else. St. Francis might have been able to "seek not to be understood but to understand," but the rest of us *need* validation, we need to feel heard. And being validated opens the door to joy.

Another way we kill the joy in others is by ignoring their efforts. Sometimes in relationships we get locked into the destructive dance of "you owe me." When two people interact with each other on the "you owe me" level, nothing the other person does is ever enough. Their efforts are never seen as a gift or an offering of love but rather as expected payment of sorts. This attitude wipes out any tender seeds of showing love to the other because it is "owed."

Sometimes we kill joy in somebody else when we ignore their efforts to change. Are you an encourager? Do you see the efforts others are making to change and grow and cheer them on? Or do you intentionally or unintentionally disregard their baby steps? We kill joy in each other when we point out how much farther they have to go rather than how far they've come. Instead, we can build joy by appreciating their efforts!

The apostle Paul was a master at showing appreciation. Every letter he wrote is full of personal greetings and words of affirmation for those who have helped him in any way. Even if they were just taking baby steps, he was so good at cheering them on. Here's just one example, from Philippians 1:5: "I thank God for the help you gave me while I preached the Good News—help you gave from the first day you believed until now" (NCV).

Ask yourself, Who is it who's been making an effort? Who has been trying and I haven't given them much encouragement? God sees our feeble efforts to grow and is pleased; let's do that for each other. Let's look for ways to say "Atta boy" or "You go, girl!" Let's not wait until they get it right or do it perfectly; let's tell them today that we see what they're doing, we appreciate it, and we're grateful for the effort. See if joy doesn't spread.

Will you pray with me?

God, I want to be someone who cheers on the efforts of others, who offers compassion when they tell me how they're feeling. I need help to do this because it does not come naturally to me. Work through me to build joy in others. In the name of Jesus, amen.

Choosing Joy Every Day

I thank you, High God—you're breathtaking!
Body and soul, I am marvelously made! I worship in adoration—what a creation!

—Psalm 139:14 MSG

Today, let's start by reminding ourselves
that *joy is a choice.* Let's remind ourselves joy is based on convictions from God's
Word—truths to believe no matter what our
circumstances are. And joy is built on emotional responses we can cultivate in our hearts
and leads to choices in our behavior.

I hope by now you are beginning to see that
the level of joy you experience is entirely in

your hands. It has very little to do with your personality or your circumstances but is based more on your understanding of joy as a gift from God and your determined choice to praise him in all things. On any given day, you get to choose how much joy you experience. It's not up to God . . . it's up to you. And it's up to me.

Those choices have to happen daily—it's nothing we can store up for the rainy days. To have joy on the rainy days, we have to choose it on the sunny days, the cloudy days, and the dark days. We must choose it daily as a gift to receive and embrace.

Read with me Romans 5:3–5: "We continue to shout our praise even when we're hemmed in with troubles, because we know how troubles can develop passionate patience in us and how that patience in turn forges the tempered steel of virtue, keeping us alert for whatever God will do next. In alert expectancy such as this, we're never left feeling shortchanged. Quite the contrary—we can't round up enough containers to hold everything God generously pours into our lives through the Holy Spirit" (MSG).

This passage reminds me that joy is a gift of the Holy Spirit. Jesus, the Man of Sorrows and the Man of Joy, came to earth and died for us so that the joy that was lost in the fall could be restored to us. And because I have the gift of joy from the Holy Spirit, I can continue to "shout my praise" even when I'm hemmed in by trouble.

Have you ever shouted praise? I grew up in and continue to be part of a rather conservative, reserved brand of Christianity that tends to frown at whoopin' and hollerin' praise. But in the last few years, in some desperate moments of pain and loss, I've shouted my praise to God, almost as an act of defiance against Satan, who loves to steal joy. Those praises were basically times when I yelled, "In your face, Satan! You cannot steal my praise!"

It becomes more than defiance, though, as I turn my eyes to God. The shouting of defiance melts into shouts of joy as I choose to gaze at God and only glance at my problems. Often this is happening through great pain, and often through tears. I didn't say it was easy—but it is possible. As William Vanderhaven says, "Life need not be easy to be joyful. Joy is not the absence of trouble but the presence of Christ."

So what are some practical behaviors to help us choose joy on a daily basis? Let's start with the three basics.

Take care of yourself. You matter. You matter to God. You matter to your family. When you believe this truth, you have a foundation for joy.

Look for a joy mentor. You and I are on a quest to develop new habits. So we need to be around people who are already choosing joy. Find a woman who, through life's ups and downs, has developed a settled assurance about God. Observe her and ask her questions.

Avoid making a big deal out of small things. It's amazing how many times it's the little annoyances that rob us of joy. As women of joy, let's deal with the small things as small things.

Today, and every day, we get to choose joy. Are you ready to take hold of your inheritance of joy? I am.

Will you pray with me?

Father, it is up to me to choose joy in my life, to embrace the birthright you have given me. I pray for wisdom to know what I can and can't control. I pray for new eyes to see all you are doing in my life. In Jesus's name, amen.

Choosing Joy
by Practicing Gratitude

Pray diligently. Stay alert, with your eyes wide open in gratitude.

—Colossians 4:2 MSG

*J*oy is not just something we think or just something we feel. At the end of the day, joy must be something we do. If joy remains at the intellectual or emotional levels without expressing itself in changed behavior, we've missed the point. Joy is not meant to just comfort us or soothe us in our pain; it is intended to become a lifestyle, an automatic response to all that comes our way.

So let's talk about how to make joy practical, doable, and attainable. For those of you who are primarily doers and are itching to have something to do, here's the part you've been waiting for!

Let's start with practicing gratitude, because a joyful heart is a grateful heart. Joy and gratitude are linked together; you can't be grateful without experiencing joy, and you can't experience joy without being grateful.

When we thank and praise God for who he is—for his worth, his Word, his works, his ways, and his will—we will find joy. When we praise and honor him for his unchangeable character in spite of crummy circumstances, our perspective changes, and we begin to see a thousand reasons to be grateful.

I don't know about you, but I tend to walk around in a fog of ingratitude—blind to the goodness of God, blind to his blessings, blind to the beauty of the world he has created. Instead of really "seeing," I waste so much emotional energy on "if only's." If only I had her husband, I could be a good wife. If only I had their children, I could be a better parent. If only we had the financial security they do, I wouldn't worry so much. In the end, these are thoughts of ingratitude, and I let them take up my time rather than appreciating what has been given to me.

In the Old Testament, there are numerous stories of people expressing gratitude to God for the ways he delivered them, took care of them, protected them, defended them, and met their needs. They didn't always get it right, but on more than one occasion they would stop along their travels and build stone monuments that would commemorate their gratitude for God's blessings on their behalf. Every person who passed by on that road from then on would have a visual reminder that God was a faithful God.

You and I are not going to build stone monuments to God's goodness and faithfulness to us—not very practical these days! But we can go outside and find an interesting rock that we can keep on our desks so that like the Israelites, when we see the rock, it will trigger the thought, *How can I express gratitude to God today?*

Maybe you would consider compiling a journal that records all the ways God has been there for you through the years—in big ways, starting with salvation, down to the tiniest, most "normal" ways, such as the breath in your lungs, and everything in between. What if you wrote down the words to songs that express your gratitude, or Scripture verses that have come to be significant in your spiritual growth? Basically you'd be writing a book of gratitude. A friend of mine keeps a gratitude journal, and every day she writes one thing for which she is grateful to God. The best part about this? On dark days when she's tempted to forget all the ways God has been good to her, she has something concrete in her hands that sets it out in black and white that God has been faithful.

And with gratitude comes joy.

Will you pray with me?

Father, every day, every moment, is a gift from you. I am grateful, and I want to remember to think on your gifts, to speak about them, to write them down. I don't want to take them for granted. Forgive me when I do, and lead me into pathways of joy today, by practicing gratitude. In Jesus's name, amen.

Choosing Joy
by Rediscovering Pleasure

> Hope in God, who richly provides us with
> everything for our enjoyment.
>
> —1 Timothy 6:17

Somehow our Christian forefathers and foremothers and early theologians have planted in our minds that pleasure is a bad thing—something we should avoid at all costs! We tend to think only worldly people seek pleasure. While it is true that pleasure out of control can lead to destructive hurts, habits, and hang-ups, there is no reason to automatically fear it, avoid it, or run from it. In fact, as 1 Timothy 6:17 says, God richly provides everything for our enjoyment. Enjoyment and pleasure are synonymous. The verse might as well have said, "God richly provides us with everything for our pleasure."

God has given us five senses by which to enjoy this world. He's given us the senses of touch, taste, sound, smell, and sight, and those senses are not just to keep us out of trouble! You don't have eyes just to keep you from bumping into the furniture. You don't have a nose just so you can avoid toxic smells. You don't have ears just to hear the ambulance coming up behind you. Our senses are not negative but totally positive, created to help us enjoy life.

I'm sure you've noticed by now that life can be very, very hard. I'd like to suggest to you that God has given us these five senses to make this challenging life more pleasant, rich, and pleasurable. There is a world of texture and taste and sight and smell and sound that we need to take advantage of. When we use our senses in that way, it releases joy.

How long has it been since you savored the taste of your favorite food? We're usually in such a hurry to fill our hunger that we inhale what's on our plates. Today, take a bite of something delicious and roll it around in your mouth and see if you can figure out all the different components that went into making it taste so good. What are the spices? What *is* that yumminess?

What if tonight you walk outside—wherever you are—and look up at the night sky? Take in the majesty of God's creation, let your eyes move from constellation to constellation, and be amazed at the world in which we live.

Take a walk tomorrow that's not for exercise but simply for getting connected to the world through your sense of hearing. Close your eyes and just listen. Hear the breeze as it whispers by your face; hear the birds singing their unique songs; hear the voices of neighbors and strangers—listen to it all.

Along with rediscovering our own pleasure in the world around us, we need to learn how to give pleasure to others—to express affection extravagantly. The Bible says in 1 Corinthians 13:13, "Love extravagantly." Most of us are not extravagant lovers; we're stingy! We dole out affection as though it were in short supply.

And yet people who touch live longer. When someone tenderly and lovingly touches us, it increases our sense of well-being. You may not have been raised in a home where affection was freely expressed or expressed appropriately, but then you of all people should know the ache in your heart that comes from a lack of physical affection. Don't let the cycle continue. Hug someone today and hold them close—savor the smell of their skin, their hair, their clothes, the feel of their skin—reconnect through the sense of touch.

We cheat ourselves out of so much available pleasure either because we think pleasure is dangerous or we're just too busy with our to-do lists to slow down and take in what our senses are telling us. And often we just don't think about it. Yet pleasure is one of God's beautiful ways for us to experience joy every day. We have only to choose it.

Will you pray with me?

Father, today I want to experience the pleasure you provide so generously. I want to live with heightened senses, ready to receive joy through taste, touch, smell, sight, and sound. I want to love extravagantly and bring pleasure to others. Help me slow down and look around. Restore my joy. In the name of Jesus, amen.

Laugh Often

Every day is a terrible day for a miserable person, but a cheerful heart has a continual feast.

—Proverbs 15:15 GW

I can't think of a better way to choose joy daily than to learn how to see the humor in life! People with "Tigger" personalities usually laugh often and easily. Those who are more laid-back and easygoing may find it easy to laugh. But for those of us who are more like Eeyore, life is serious business. Life is intense; those train tracks of sorrow regularly overtake our joy. And those of you who are task-oriented may find that your efforts to get things done efficiently or quickly cause you to miss the humor in life. But to increase your daily joy, you need to learn how to laugh!

If we're honest, we have to admit that life is basically absurd—full of ridiculous moments in which all we can do is laugh. That's why *America's Funniest Home Videos* has had such a long run on TV! We love to laugh at the stupid things other people do and the mishaps that happen to them. The show capitalizes on the concept that life is absurd and you might as well laugh about it.

Through the ages, some have understood that life is absurd but have chosen to concentrate on the pain and sadness life brings. And they've decided that because there is pain and sadness in life, God must not exist. I believe that because life is absurd and there is pain, I need God more than ever. Yes, there is pain. But we run *to* God in our pain, not away from him.

I remember reading that laughter and tears come from the same deep well inside us. That's why sometimes you can laugh until you cry. And sometimes we cry until we laugh. If you can laugh but can't cry, think about it. If you can cry but can't laugh, think about it. If you can do neither, consider talking to a Christian friend or counselor, because we were made to both laugh and cry.

Choosing joy means we choose to find the humor in life. Then we have a continual feast every day, as Proverbs 15:15 says.

Because I'm an Eeyore, I have to practice finding humor more than other people—it's pretty hard to make me belly laugh. My whole family can watch a movie together and everyone will be laughing at the inane actions of the movie characters except me. I'm famous in my family for barely cracking a smile. They consider it a huge victory—an Oscar-worthy movie—if Mom laughs aloud! Sad, isn't it?

And it's totally ironic because I'm married to a man who lives to make me laugh. Rick is not above sticking pencils in his nose or doing pratfalls like Steve Carell just to get a giggle out of me. In my car, I listen to the clean comedy channel when I'm driving—not because I'm bored but so I can practice laughing and improve my sense of humor! Crazy, huh? Yet at least I'm doing something to choose joy. What do you need to do to laugh more?

Maybe you need to do some soul work. Ask yourself—why is laughter difficult for me? It might be because you're more reserved. But what if underneath it all is an attitude of judging, of finding others' efforts to be lacking and therefore not "worthy" of your approval through laughter? We're complicated people, that's for sure. It's worth thinking about, because seeing the humor in life's absurdities is one of the ways we can choose joy. I want a continual feast, don't you?

Will you pray with me?

God, today will bring moments so absurd I can only laugh or cry. Help me to find the humor in my day and to laugh. I know you are with me, whether the day holds sadness or happiness. So today I choose to laugh often. In Jesus's name, amen.

Lighten Someone's Load

Therefore as we have opportunity, let us do good to all people, especially to those who belong to the family of believers.

—Galatians 6:10

On this journey to increasing the joy in our lives, there is one very obvious way to choose joy every day: become a giver instead of a taker. Find the delight in giving and serving.

You've probably seen the bumper sticker that says, "Practice random acts of kindness." I like that, even though it's cheesy. What if as Christ-followers we took that secular thought and began to apply it in our daily lives? What if we actively looked for ways to lighten someone else's load?

Most of the time we go about our business with a bit of an attitude. We have an imaginary hand held out in front of us, acting like a protective shield, one that keeps others from bothering us too much, getting in our way, or interrupting our carefully orchestrated schedule. We figure if we keep that hand out in front, our heads lowered, and our eyes down, we won't have to make contact with anyone who might mess with our plans.

Of course, everybody has days that are just packed to the brim. But we're talking about an attitude that becomes a pattern—a way of life—in which we start to think everyone exists to serve us, to meet our needs, to help us get our tasks done, and to make our lives easier. Everyone from waiters to grocery store checkers to bank tellers is there for us; and if they're slower than suits us, or fumble something, or make a mistake, or make us wait longer than we think is appropriate, we're likely to become nothing but a big fat taker.

Sometimes we go a different route. We decide that all we have and possess is ours. We become like the seagulls in *Finding Nemo*, shrieking "Mine! Mine! Mine!" We ease our consciences by saying things like "I will become a giver someday."

Second Corinthians 8:1–4 tells a different story of following Christ. The Macedonian church gave out of their abject poverty with "overflowing joy." They were suffering extreme poverty, and yet when they heard about brothers and sisters in Jerusalem who were in need, they took up an offering and sent it to them. The result? Overflowing joy. It is no accident that in giving when they themselves had nothing, they experienced overflowing joy.

Maybe you are in abject emotional poverty, overwhelmed by your own trials. Commit to spend fifteen minutes listening to someone else's hurts; give to them what you need to receive. Maybe you're in abject physical poverty, worn to the bone by weariness and fatigue. Offer to run an errand for a neighbor who needs a hand. Maybe you're in abject financial poverty, not sure where the money will come from to pay the bills. Buy a can of soup and give it to someone else.

Don't wait to become a giver. Don't wait until you have more strength. Don't wait until you have more time. Don't wait until you have more money. Lighten someone else's load; become a giver. And just like the Macedonian church who gave out of their nothingness, watch overflowing joy fill your soul!

Will you pray with me?

God, please forgive me for being so consumed with my own needs, my own wants. I want to be a giver, even when I'm feeling overwhelmed myself. Help me look at the world as a giver today, finding places to lighten the load of someone else. In Jesus's name, amen.

Finding Joy Mentors

Bad friends will ruin good habits.

—1 Corinthians 15:33 NCV

As we start some new habits—habits that will lead us to a richer experience of joy in our lives—one of the best decisions we can make is to intentionally seek out joyful people. Being around sour, negative people all the time will put a serious dent in our own level of joy. There's a lot of truth to the saying "misery loves company." Studies have shown that living with a depressed person eventually begins to affect the other members of a household, leading many of them to also begin to become depressed.

Why? While depression isn't a virus or a bacteria that you can spread to someone else by contact, it is an emotional "virus" that slowly creeps in and begins to take others down. The constant depressed mood and thinking of those suffering from severe depression definitely is "catching." Please don't misunderstand me and think I'm saying that if you have a family member or a close friend who is struggling with depression that you should minimize contact with them or dump them . . . not at all! All I'm saying is that you need to counterbalance the impact on your life by also being with people who are joyful.

John Ortberg says we should all look for joy mentors—people who are further down the road who exhibit a strong, positive faith in God's goodness and faithfulness, and who make it a regular practice to praise God, even in the roughest of times. He says we need to get to know them and find out what they have learned that has allowed them to choose joy no matter what.

This doesn't need to be a formal arrangement. Find a joy mentor and watch them.

133

Observe them in different situations so that you can determine how they choose joy, no matter what the circumstance!

In addition to more mature joy mentors, some of the sweetest joy mentors are children! Nobody has a better sense of humor than small children. They will laugh at anything! You make funny sounds, they laugh. You make strange faces, they laugh. They are playful, they giggle, they smile, they find pleasure in cardboard boxes and bits of string. Children have a sense of wonder; everything is new to them, and they ask endless questions about the world around them. Their curiosity is unquenchable, and their delight in being tickled and hugged and squeezed and giving sweet kisses is almost more joy than I can handle!

I realize that not all of you are parents and not all of you are even aunts or uncles, and you might live quite a distance from the little children you are related to. It doesn't matter. Children are everywhere . . . and everyone needs at least one child in their lives to teach them again how to experience joy. Talk to a neighbor's child, wave at a baby in the grocery store, laugh with toddlers in a restaurant instead of frowning at them, or volunteer for the child care at your church. Do something that lets the joy that children have rub off on you. When you choose to be around joyful people, watch the joy begin to sprout again in you!

Will you pray with me?

Father, open my eyes today and help me see the joyful people around me. Help me watch and learn from them, laugh with them, and move further myself down the path of choosing joy daily. In Jesus's name, amen.

Living in the Moment

Make the most of every opportunity.

—Ephesians 5:16 (NLT)

Sometimes the most powerful way we can choose joy daily is to live in the moment. Notice I said live *in* the moment, not live *for* the moment—those are very different things. To live for the moment is irresponsible and can lead to some rash decisions you'll regret forever. Living in the moment is totally responsible. It's when we live wisely, recognizing that every moment in our lives is worth cherishing.

As a perfectionist, I'm always waiting for a perfect moment before I enjoy it—except that nothing is ever perfect, right? Because perfection is not difficult, it's impossible. Which means there is no such thing as the "perfect moment." So if I'm going to cherish the moments of my life with the people in my life and the times of my life, I have to do it now . . . imperfect though it may be.

We spend too much time regretting the unrepeatable past and wishing we could get a "do over." Or we waste our energy on worry and anxiety about the unknowable future. Either way, today is ignored or minimized.

A friend of mine has a daughter with severe cerebral palsy. She told me one day she and her husband decided to take their young daughter out of her wheelchair and put her on the floor so she could be with her four siblings. Meagan is very stiff and has almost no ability to control her movements, so to put her down on the floor with her rough and tough siblings was risky. They were laughing and tickling and being loud, as usual. But when they laid her on the floor near her brother and sisters, a smile as wide as Texas spread across her face, and her delight in being able to be in the heap of goofy siblings was palpable. My friend said to herself, "I'm loving this moment!"

Did they have to put their daughter back in the wheelchair in a few minutes? Yes. Did playing on the ground with her siblings change her physical condition? No. Did it take away the sting of limitations or pain or hardship? No. But when my friend opened up her heart to live in the moment, she opened up her heart to joy.

In Psalm 118:24 we read, "This is the day the LORD has made. We will rejoice and be glad in it" (NLT).

Every single word of this verse brings meaning to us joy-seekers. Let's say it again, emphasizing a different word each time. *This* is the day that the Lord has made. This *is* the day that the Lord has made. This is the *day* that the Lord has made. This is the day that the *Lord* has made. This is the day that the Lord has *made* . . . I *will* rejoice and be glad in it.

If you want to exponentially increase the level of joy in your life, you must choose to start living in the moments of your life. Stop waiting for perfect conditions. Stop waiting for all the little ducks to get in a row. Stop waiting for everything to be exactly the way you think it should be. Enjoy this moment, even if this moment contains pain and sorrow. It is in this moment that the Lord can be found, and where he is, there is joy.

Will you pray with me?

Father, I thank you for this moment. I thank you for your presence, the gift of being with you in this moment. I choose to rejoice in today, and experience it as fully as possible, with your help. In the name of Jesus, amen.

Finding the Bless in the Mess

Whatever is true, whatever is noble, whatever is right, whatever is pure, whatever is lovely, whatever is admirable—if anything is excellent or praiseworthy—think about such things.

—Philippians 4:8

A few years ago I heard a professional stress consultant say that one of the ways to decrease stress and increase joy was to find the "bless in the mess"—that hidden inside every mess is a blessing. I totally agree.

Remember, life is not like hills and valleys with moments of joy and then moments of sorrow; it's much more like parallel train tracks where joy and sorrow are linked and run side by side throughout our lives. So in every circumstance, to choose joy, we must learn how to find the bless in the mess; how to sift through the sorrow to find the joy.

Corrie ten Boom was a Dutch woman who hid Jews from the Nazis during WWII. She and her family were eventually betrayed by Nazi sympathizers. Corrie, her sister, Betsy, and their father, as well as some of the people they had been hiding, were sent to concentration camps. Corrie and Betsy wanted to lead a Bible study for the women in their barracks, but they were fearful the guards would discover what they were doing. Corrie was complaining pretty heavily one day, complaining that God had let them be arrested and imprisoned in the first place, and then complaining about the lice that covered them all. Betsy had a different perspective. "Corrie," she said, "we need to praise God! The blessing is that the guards don't want to come in because of the lice! We get to share the love of Jesus Christ with these hurting women unhindered because of the lice!"

Betsy found the bless in the mess.

In my own life, I've discovered the bless in the mess of marriage problems. Rick and I are total opposites in just about every way possible, and that has made for some very interesting moments in our years together. It has led to a lot of conflict and times when we have to forgive each other one more time and choose reconciliation and unity and harmony in spite of the different ways we look at life. But the blessing is that because we know what it's like to have to work hard to build a strong marriage, we are able to encourage other couples who are ready to give up. Our struggle allows us to enter into their pain and offer hope.

I was molested as a very young girl by someone our family knew. I kept it a secret for many years, in denial of the "cost" of what happened and how it affected me. That's the mess. But when I stopped living in denial and got help, God healed much of the brokenness that had resulted. The bless in the mess is the connection I have with other women who have suffered sexual abuse; I get to tell them that if God healed me, he can heal them too.

I've had breast cancer and melanoma—that's definitely a mess. But the blessing in the mess is the way I can identify with people who receive a life-threatening diagnosis. I too know what it is like to have a doctor sit with you and talk about life expectancy charts and statistical odds. Our shared mess creates a link between my heart and theirs. We understand each other—the fears, the anxieties, the questions that come with illness.

It is from the messes that ministry comes. God did not allow the messes in your life capriciously or needlessly. Some of them you brought on yourself; some of them came unexpectedly like a rogue wind. But God has allowed them; now it's up to you to look for the bless in the mess.

Will you pray with me?

Father, help me find the blessings hidden in the broken places, so that my joy will grow. Help me to trust you to use and redeem the messy parts of my life, turning them into ministry. In the name of Jesus, amen.

The Decision
to Choose Joy

May the God of hope fill you with all joy
and peace as you trust in him, so that you
may overflow with hope by the power of the
Holy Spirit.

—Romans 15:13

*D*o you remember the definition of joy I
gave at the beginning of this book? Joy
is the settled assurance that God is in control
of all the details of my life, the quiet confidence that ultimately everything is going to be
all right, and the determined choice to praise
him in all things.

Joy is not about feeling happy all the time. Joy is a settled assurance *about* God, a quiet confidence *in* God, and a determined choice to give my praise *to* God.

We've talked about how trials put our faith-life on display for a watching world to evaluate, and what is exposed isn't always very pretty. You may have discovered your faith-life wasn't nearly as strong or stable as you thought it was, and that can be shocking and disappointing.

We've talked about building joy on the truths about God—who he is and how he never changes. And because he never changes, he will be there for us when the people we were counting on don't show up; when the places we live don't satisfy; when the possessions get lost or broken; when the position is given to someone else; and when our personalities aren't enough to take us through the tough times.

The truth is, God is the only source of joy for me . . . and for you. We can try to use our own efforts to find joy and quench our thirsty souls, but all of our efforts only lead to more frustration, because there's no way we can ever build lives on our own that will hold joy . . . they're broken.

We've looked at the attitudes of our hearts—the ways that we kill joy in ourselves and in others, and how we can move from being joy-killers to becoming joy-builders.

We've been digging into the practical ways of choosing joy on a daily basis—practicing gratitude, rediscovering pleasure through our senses, expressing affection extravagantly, seeing the humor in life, befriending joyful people, becoming a giver instead of a taker, living in the moment, and deciding to look for the blessings hidden in the messes of our existence.

It's possible that you have read these devotions and have realized that you don't personally know Jesus Christ, the Man of Joy. You've heard about him, you even admire him, but you don't know him. Today is your day! Pray a simple prayer—the words don't matter nearly as much as the attitude of your heart. Say something like, "Jesus, I'm tired of living my life on my own. I want to know you, to be a part of your family. I'm asking you to save me from my sins and teach me how to follow you the rest of my life."

And now it all boils down to this statement: for you to experience joy in your life, it will be in spite of your circumstances, in the middle of your trials, even if things don't work out like you hope. Ask yourself, *What unchangeable circumstance stands in the way of my choosing joy? What would it look like for me to choose joy in spite of it?* Then ask yourself, *What is happening right now that may or may not change? What would it look like for me to choose joy in the middle of this trial?* Then ask, *What fears for the future might keep me from choosing joy? What if this or that happens? Will I choose joy then?*

This is not a perfect world; we know that. So if you wait for the perfect day, the perfect moment, the perfect opportunity, the perfect vacation, the perfect job, the perfect relationship—you'll wait forever. You'll miss joy. Remember, you were created for joy, and if you miss it, you'll miss the reason for your existence. You have to take a hard look at God, at yourself, at your circumstances. And then, in spite of, in the middle of, and even if what you fear comes true, you make a decision to choose joy.

Say it with me: I choose joy! I choose joy! I CHOOSE JOY.

Will you pray with me?

Now to you, Father, who are able to do immeasurably more than all we ask or imagine, to you be glory for ever and ever! Amen.

Finding Joy and Hope in the Word of God

*I*n the past few years, I've clung even more to the Word of God as I seek to choose joy daily. May these words be a source of strength and hope to you as well.

- "Whatever happens, dear friends, be glad in the LORD. I never get tired of telling you this, and it is good for you to hear it again and again" (Phil. 3:1 TLB).

- "Nothing is as wonderful as knowing Christ Jesus my Lord. I have given up everything else and count it all as garbage. All I want is Christ" (Phil. 3:8 CEV).

- I have strength for all things in Christ Who empowers me. I am ready for anything and equal to anything through Him Who infuses inner strength into me; I am self-sufficient in Christ's sufficiency. (Phil. 4:13 AMP).

- "Those who sow in tears will reap with songs of joy, he who goes out weeping, carrying seed to sow, will return with songs of joy, carrying sheaves with him" (Ps. 126:5–6).

- "I wait quietly before God, for my hope is in him. He alone is my rock and my salvation, my fortress where I will not be shaken" (Ps. 62:5–6).

- "Be happy with what you have because God has said, 'I will never abandon you or leave you'" (Heb. 13:5 GW).

- "I will sing joyful praises and be filled with excitement like a guest at a banquet. I think about you before I go to sleep, and my thoughts turn to you during the night" (Ps. 63:5–6 CEV).

- "His anger lasts only a moment, but his favor lasts a lifetime! Weeping may last through the night, but joy comes with the morning" (Ps. 30:5 NLT).

- "Restore to me the joy of your salvation and grant me a willing spirit, to sustain me" (Ps. 51:12).

- "When anxiety was great within me, your consolation brought me joy" (Ps. 94:19).

- "Why, my soul, are you downcast? Why so disturbed within me? Put your hope in God, for I will yet praise him, my Savior and my God" (Ps. 43:5).

- "I pray that the eyes of your heart may be enlightened in order that you may know the hope to which he has called you, the riches of his glorious inheritance in his holy people" (Eph. 1:18).

- "I consider that our present sufferings are not worth comparing with the glory that will be revealed in us" (Rom. 8:18).

- "We pray that you'll have the strength to stick it out over the long haul—not the grim strength of gritting your teeth but the glory-strength God gives. It is strength that endures the unendurable and spills over into joy" (Col. 1:11 MSG).

- "When they walk through the Valley of Weeping, it will become a place of refreshing springs. The autumn rains will clothe it with blessings" (Ps. 84:6 NLT).

- "A thief is only there to steal and kill and destroy. I came so they can have real and eternal life, more and better life than they ever dreamed of" (John 10:10 MSG).

- "I have told you these things, so that in me you may have peace. In this world you will have trouble. But take heart! I have overcome the world" (John 16:33).

- "I cried out to the Lord in my suffering, and he heard me. He set me free from all my fears" (Ps. 34:6 NLT).

- "My body and mind may waste away, but God remains the foundation of my life

and my inheritance forever" (Ps. 73:26
GW).

- "Be glad for all God is planning for you.
  Be patient . . . and always be prayerful"
  (Rom. 12:12 NLT).

Kay Warren, cofounder with her husband, Rick, of Saddleback Church in Lake Forest, California, is a Bible teacher, an international speaker, and a bestselling author. Warren is a respected advocate for those living with HIV and AIDS, orphaned and vulnerable children, as well as for those affected by a mental illness. She founded Saddleback's HIV & AIDS Initiative. Kay is the author of *Sacred Privilege* and *Say Yes to God* and coauthor of *Foundations*, a popular systematic theology course used by churches worldwide. Her children are Amy and Josh, and Matthew who is in Heaven, and she has five grandchildren. Learn more at www .kaywarren.com, and follow her on Facebook (Kay Warren) and on Twitter (@KayWarren1).

Perfect *for* Small Groups!

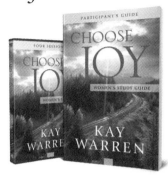

In this *Choose Joy* four-session video-based study, Kay Warren encourages you to examine your beliefs and choices about happiness and joy. In her honest and engaging style, she will challenge you to consider new ways of thinking, feeling, and acting that allow joy to take root and grow, even in the darkest times. In the *Choose Joy Women's Study Guide*, small group questions are provided to enhance discussion, meditation, and personal application.

Choose Joy DVD Curriculum and Participant's Guide Include:

Session One: Jesus, Man of Joy
Session Two: Joy Is a Conviction of My Mind
Session Three: Joy Is a Condition of My Heart
Session Four: Joy Is a Choice of My Behavior

 Revell
a division of Baker Publishing Group
www.RevellBooks.com

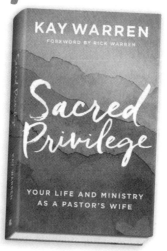